TEXAS ROADHOUSE C

RECIPES

Replicate The Most Wanted Recipes From Your Favorite Restaurant At Home

By Elena Harris

Contents

Introduction

Texas Roadhouse, you must have heard about the place and tried a number of its delicious meals, and that makes the most of us, as the food chain is working in different parts of the world. In the USA along Texas Roadhouse is running in 593 different location. This American Western-themed food chain offers you the best steaks in town, and it specializes in the loss of other meals as well. The Texas Roadhouse started off its journey from Clarksville, Indiana, then spread its magical flavors all around. As of today, the chain has it's headquartered in Louisville, Kentucky, and you can find its outlets serving you the quality, not only in 49 states of USA but in a number of other countries including Kuwait, Bahrain, Saudi Arabia, UAE, Qatar, Philippines, Taiwan, South Korea, And Mexico. Perhaps, the entire gulf and Americas has millions of Texas Roadhouse fans who love to have its delectable delights every now and then. It has been 27 years since the Texas Roadhouse came into existence, and every new generation falls harder for its classic flavors than the generations before. It is this popularity of this food chain and my personal fondness of the Texas Roadhouse meals that made me recreate all its delicious dishes at home. And these recipes are not only delightful to eat, but you can have the best time cooking them at home too.

This cookbook provides a comprehensive Texas Roadhouse menu with all the recipes that you can make and serve on all the special occasions and as your routine meals as well. From crispy snacks to complete entrees, combos, burgers, salads, drinks, and desserts, there is every special recipe from this restaurant chain. Now you don't need to order or dine out every time you feel like eating from Texas Roadhouse because this book brings all the secrets behind the Texas Roadhouse unique flavors down to your kitchen floors. It has easy recipes with basic ingredients, which you can bring together to create an entire Texas Roadhouse Copycat menu at home. Trust me! This menu will make you popular among your friends and family. The finger-licking meals from this cookbook will keep them spellbound for hours, and everyone will be amazed by the Texas Roadhouse-like taste.

So, if you want to cook like professionals and like enjoy the authentic Texas Roadhouse flavors at home, then continue reading, as we are about to share all the copycat recipes from this world-renown American restaurant chain.

Espresso Steak

Serves: 2
Nutritional Information (per serving):
Calories: 216 | Carbs: 4g | Fats: 12g | Protein: 22g

Ingredients

- 3 teaspoons instant espresso powder
- 2 teaspoons brown sugar
- 1-1/2 teaspoons smoked paprika
- 1 teaspoon salt
- 1 teaspoon baking cocoa
- 1/4 teaspoon pumpkin pie spice
- 1/4 teaspoon pepper
- 1-lb. (3/4-inch-thick) beef flat iron

Directions:

1. Set the oven broiler on medium heat.
2. Mix espresso powder, brown sugar, paprika, salt, cocoa, spice, and pepper in a bowl.
3. Liberally rub this espresso mixture over the steak and place it in a baking pan.
4. Leave these steaks for 10 minutes for marination.
5. Broil the marinated steak for 6 minutes per side.
6. Slice and serve warm.

Texas Red Chili

Serves: 6
Nutritional Information (per serving):
Calories: 359 | Carbs: 26g | Fats: 18g | Protein: 23g

Ingredients

- 1 can (28 oz.) diced tomatoes, undrained
- 1 can (15 oz.) black beans, drained
- 1 can (15 oz.) kidney beans, rinsed and drained
- 1 lb. boneless beef chuck steak, cut into cubes
- 1 lb. bulk spicy pork sausage, cooked and drained
- 2 medium onions, chopped
- 1 medium sweet red pepper, chopped
- 1 medium green pepper, chopped
- 1 cup hot chunky salsa
- 1/3 cup medium pearl barley

Directions:

1. Add tomatoes, black beans, kidney beans, steak, pork sausage, onions, red pepper, green pepper, chunky salad, and barley to a slow cooker.
2. Cover the chili mixture and cook for 8 hours on Low Heat.
3. Mix well and serve warm.

Beef Tips with Mushroom Sauce

Serves: 4
Nutritional Information (per serving):
Calories: 278 | Carbs: 12g | Fats: 10g | Protein: 32g

Ingredients

- 1/4 teaspoon black pepper
- 3 teaspoons olive oil
- 1 (1 lb.) beef top sirloin steak, cubed
- 1/3 cup dry red wine
- 1/2 lb. sliced baby portobello mushrooms
- 1 small onion, halved and sliced
- 1/2 teaspoon salt
- 2 cups beef broth
- 1 tablespoon Worcestershire sauce
- 3 to 4 tablespoons cornstarch
- 1/4 cup cold water
- Hot cooked pasta

Directions:

1. Pour olive oil into a 6-quart pressure cooker and heat it on sauté mode.
2. Place beef in it, season it with salt and black pepper, then sear until brown.
3. Transfer this seared meat to a plate and keep it aside.
4. Add wine to the cooker and deglaze the cooker.
5. Stir in onion, broth, mushrooms, and Worcestershire sauce.
6. Mix well and return the beef to the cooker.
7. Seal the pressure cooker's lid and cook for 15 minutes on high heat.
8. Release the steam and remove the lid.
9. Switch the cooker to Sauté mode. Mix cornstarch with water in a bowl.
10. Pour this slurry into the cooker and cook the beef until its sauce thickens.
11. Serve warm with pasta.

Grilled Chicken with Arugula Salad

Serves: 6
Nutritional Information (per serving):
Calories: 204 | Carbs: 14.5g | Fats: 5.8g | Protein: 27.3g

Ingredients

- 2/3 cup 2 tablespoons olive oil
- 1/4 cup shallots, finely chopped
- 1/4 cup champagne vinegar
- 1 teaspoon salt
- 1/2 teaspoon pepper
- 1/2 lb. baby portobello mushrooms, sliced
- 1/2 lb. fresh mushrooms, sliced
- 4 (6 oz.) chicken breast halves, boneless
- 6 cups fresh baby arugula
- 1/2 cup Parmesan cheese, shredded

Directions:

1. Add shallots, 2/3 cup oil, vinegar, ¼ teaspoon pepper, ½ teaspoon salt to a blender.
2. Press the pulse button and blend for 30 seconds.
3. Keep 3 tablespoons of this dressing and pour the rest into a large bowl.
4. Stir in mushrooms and mix to coat well. Leave them to marinate for 5 minutes.
5. Set a grill over medium heat and grease its grilling grates.
6. Grill the coated and marinated mushrooms for 5 minutes per side.
7. Brush the chicken with remaining oil, and season with black pepper and salt.
8. Grill the spices chicken for 8 minutes per side.
9. Toss the arugula leaves with grilled mushrooms, reserve vinaigrette, and cheese in a bowl.
10. Serve this salad with grilled chicken.
11. Serve warm.

Fried Pickles

Serves: 8
Nutritional Information (per serving):
Calories: 65 | Carbs: 9g | Fats: 2g | Protein: 3g

Ingredients

- 32 dill pickle slices
- 1/2 cup all-purpose flour
- 1/2 teaspoon salt
- 2 large eggs, lightly beaten
- 2 tablespoons dill pickle juice
- 1/2 teaspoon cayenne pepper
- 1/2 teaspoon garlic powder
- 1/2 cup panko bread crumbs
- 1 tablespoon snipped fresh dill

Directions:

1. At 500 degrees F, preheat your oven.
2. Drain and dry the pickles by placing them in a plate lined with a paper towel. Leave them for 15 minutes.
3. Meanwhile, mix flour with salt in one shallow bowl.
4. Beat eggs with cayenne, garlic powder, and pickle juice in a bowl.
5. Mix panko with dill in another shallow tray.
6. First, coat the pickles with flour mixture, dip them in the eggs, and coat with panko mixture.
7. Place the pickles on a wire rack and set the rack on a baking sheet.
8. Bake the pickles for 25 minutes in the oven until golden brown.
9. Serve warm.

Bacon and Garlic Green Beans

Serves: 10
Nutritional Information (per serving):
Calories: 176 | Carbs: 7g | Fats: 14g | Protein: 4g

Ingredients

- 6 thick-sliced bacon strips, chopped
- 1 small onion, thinly sliced
- 6 tablespoons butter
- 1 tablespoon olive oil
- 3 garlic cloves, minced
- 1/4 cup white wine
- 9 cups French-style green beans
- 1/2 teaspoon salt
- 1/2 teaspoon garlic powder
- 1/4 teaspoon black pepper
- 2 to 3 tablespoons lemon juice

Directions:

1. Set a large skillet over medium heat.
2. Add bacon and sauté until bacon is crispy.
3. Transfer the bacon on top of a plate lined with a paper towel.
4. Add butter and onion to the same skillet and sauté until soft.
5. Stir in garlic and sauté for 1 minute.
6. Pour in the wine and cook to a boil. Then reduce the heat to a simmer.
7. Cook for 8 minutes and add salt, garlic powder, green beans, and black pepper.
8. Mix and cook for 7 minutes. Stir in bacon and lemon juice.
9. Serve warm.

Spicy Chicken Wings with Blue Cheese Dip

Serves: 6
Nutritional Information (per serving):
Calories: 273 | Carbs: 4g | Fats: 19g | Protein: 11g

Ingredients

- 1 cup reduced-sodium soy sauce
- 2/3 cup sugar
- 2 teaspoons salt
- 2 teaspoons grated orange zest
- 2 garlic cloves, minced
- 1/2 teaspoon pepper
- 3 lbs. chicken wingettes
- 3 teaspoons chili powder
- 3/4 teaspoon cayenne pepper
- 3/4 teaspoon hot pepper sauce

BLUE CHEESE DIP

- 1 cup mayonnaise
- 1/2 cup blue cheese salad dressing
- 1/3 cup buttermilk
- 2 teaspoons Italian salad dressing mix

Directions:

1. Mix soy sauce, salt, sugar, orange zest, black pepper, and garlic in a small bowl.
2. Transfer half of this marinade to another shallow dish.
3. Add chicken to this marinate, mix well, cover, and refrigerate for 1 hour.
4. Cover the remaining marinade and refrigerate.
5. Remove the juicy marinated chicken from the marinade and transfer to a 13x9 inches baking dish.
6. Cover this chicken dish and bake for 1 ½ hour in the oven at 325 degrees F
7. Transfer this chicken to another 15x10 inches baking pan.
8. Add cayenne, pepper sauce, and chili powder to the reserved marinade.
9. Mix well and pour over the chicken evenly.
10. Bake for another 30 minutes in the oven.
11. Meanwhile, prepare the blue cheese dip by blending all its ingredients in a blender.
12. Serve baked chicken with blue cheese dip.

Cajun Baked Catfish

Serves: 2
Nutritional Information (per serving):
Calories: 242 | Carbs: 8g | Fats: 10g | Protein: 27g

Ingredients

- 2 tablespoons yellow cornmeal
- 2 teaspoons Cajun or blackened seasoning
- 1/2 teaspoon dried thyme
- 1/2 teaspoon dried basil
- 1/4 teaspoon garlic powder
- 1/4 teaspoon lemon-pepper seasoning
- 2 (6 oz.) catfish or tilapia fillets
- 1/4 teaspoon paprika

Directions:

1. At 400 degrees F, preheat your oven.
2. Mix cornmeal, Cajun seasoning, thyme, basil, garlic powder, and lemon-pepper seasoning in a bowl.
3. Coat the tilapia fillet with cornmeal mixture and place them in a greased baking sheet.
4. Drizzle paprika on top and bake for 25 minutes.
5. Serve warm.

Balsamic Steak Salad

Serves: 4
Nutritional Information (per serving):
Calories: 151 | Carbs: 6g | Fats: 9g | Protein: 12g

Ingredients

- 1/4 cup balsamic vinegar
- 1/4 cup olive oil
- 1 teaspoon fresh thyme, minced
- 1/4 teaspoon salt
- 1/8 teaspoon coarsely ground pepper
- 1 (3/4 lb.) beef flat iron steak
- 2 teaspoons lemon juice
- 1 package (9 oz.) ready-to-serve salad greens
- 8 cherry tomatoes, halved
- 4 radishes, cut into slices
- 1/2 ripe avocado, peeled and sliced
- 1/4 cup dried cranberries
- Crumbled blue cheese and additional pepper

Directions:

1. Blend balsamic vinegar, olive oil, lemon juice, thyme, salt, and black pepper in a bowl to make the marinade.
2. Pour ¼ cup dressing into a Ziplock bag and place the steak in it.
3. Seal the bag, shake and refrigerate for 8 hours or more. Store the remaining marinade.
4. Set a grill over medium heat and grease its grilling grates.
5. Grill the beefsteak for 8 minutes per side then slice.
6. Mix the remaining marinade with greens, tomatoes, radishes, avocado, and cranberries in a bowl.
7. Divide the cranberries salad between the plates and serve the steak on top.
8. Garnish with black pepper and cheese.
9. Serve.

Road Kill Steak

Serves: 4
Nutritional Information (per serving):
Calories: 358 | Carbs: 2g | Fats: 21g | Protein: 36g

Ingredients

- 4 (6 oz.) beef tenderloin steaks
- 1 teaspoon steak seasoning
- 2 tablespoons butter
- 1 cup sliced fresh mushrooms
- 1/2 cup reduced-sodium beef broth
- 1/4 cup heavy whipping cream
- 1 tablespoon steak sauce
- 1 teaspoon garlic salt with parsley
- 1 teaspoon minced chives

Directions:

1. Liberally rub the steaks with steak seasoning.
2. Set a large-sized skillet over medium heat.
3. Add butter to the hot skillet and sear the steak in the melted butter for 5 minutes per side.
4. Transfer the cooked and seared steak to a plate and keep it aside.
5. Add mushrooms to the same skillet and sauté until soft.
6. Pour in broth, cream, garlic salt, and steak sauce.
7. Mix well, boil, and cook for 2 minutes until thickens.
8. Return the steaks to a sauce and garnish with chives.
9. Serve warm.

Tater Skins

Serves: 8
Nutritional Information (per serving):
Calories: 313 | Carbs: 17g | Fats: 23g | Protein: 11g

Ingredients

- 4 large baking potatoes, baked
- 3 tablespoons canola oil
- 1 tablespoon grated Parmesan cheese
- 1/2 teaspoon salt
- 1/4 teaspoon garlic powder
- 1/4 teaspoon paprika
- 1/8 teaspoon pepper
- 8 bacon strips, cooked and crumbled
- 1-1/2 cups shredded cheddar cheese
- 1/2 cup sour cream
- 4 green onions, sliced

Directions:

1. At 475 degrees F, preheat the oven.
2. Cut the potatoes in half, lengthwise. Remove its pulp from the center while leaving ¼ inches shell.
3. Place these potato skins in a greased baking sheet.
4. Mix canola oil, parmesan cheese, salt, garlic powder, paprika, black pepper, bacon, cheddar cheese, sour cream in a mixing bowl.
5. Divide this mixture into the potato skins and bake for 7 minutes.
6. Garnish with green onions.
7. Serve warm.

Mushroom-Stuffed Cheeseburgers

Serves: 8
Nutritional Information (per serving):
Calories: 418 | Carbs: 33g | Fats: 17g | Protein: 31g

Ingredients

- 2 bacon strips, finely chopped
- 2 cups chopped fresh mushrooms
- 1/4 cup chopped onion
- 1/4 cup chopped sweet red pepper
- 1/4 cup chopped green pepper
- 2 lbs. lean ground beef (90% lean)
- 2 tablespoons steak sauce
- 1/2 teaspoon seasoned salt
- 4 slices provolone cheese, halved
- 8 Kaiser rolls, split

Directions:

1. Set a large iron skillet over medium heat and sauté bacon until crispy.
2. Transfer to a plate lined with paper towels.
3. Add pepper, mushrooms, and onion to the same pan and sauté until soft.
4. Transfer the mixture to a bowl and add bacon.
5. Mix beef with salt and steak sauce in a bowl.
6. Make 16 thin patties out of this mixture.
7. Place eight patties on the working surface.
8. Top them with cheese and mushroom mixture and place the remaining patties on top.
9. Press the edges of all the patties together to seal the filling inside.
10. Preheat a grill over medium heat and grease its grilling grates.
11. Grill the stuffed burgers for 6 minutes per side.
12. Serve warm.

Barbecued Chicken

Serves: 6
Nutritional Information (per serving):
Calories: 370 | Carbs: 15g | Fats: 19g | Protein: 33g

Ingredients

- 2 (3 lbs.) broiler chickens, cut into 8 pieces
- Salt and black pepper, to taste

BARBECUE SAUCE

- 2 tablespoons canola oil
- 2 small onions, finely chopped
- 2 cups ketchup
- 1/4 cup lemon juice
- 2 tablespoons brown sugar
- 2 tablespoons water
- 1 teaspoon ground mustard
- 1/2 teaspoon garlic powder
- 1/4 teaspoon pepper
- 1/8 teaspoon salt
- 1/8 teaspoon hot pepper sauce

Directions:

1. Season the chicken pieces with black pepper and salt.
2. Set a grill over medium heat and grease its grilling grates.
3. Grill the chicken pieces in the grill for 20 minutes per side.
4. Set a small saucepan over medium heat and sauté onion with oil until soft.
5. Stir in all the sauce ingredients, cook it to a boil and let it simmer for 10 minutes.
6. Brush the half-grilled chicken with barbecue sauce and flip to grill for 25 minutes.
7. Continue basting the chicken with BBQ sauce every 10 minutes.
8. Serve warm.

Balsamic-Glazed Beef Skewers

Serves: 4
Nutritional Information (per serving):
Calories: 194 | Carbs: 7g | Fats: 7g | Protein: 25g

Ingredients

- 1 lb. beef top sirloin steak, diced into cubes
- 1 teaspoon Dijon mustard
- 1/4 cup barbecue sauce
- 1/4 cup balsamic vinaigrette
- 2 cups cherry tomatoes

Directions:

1. Mix balsamic vinaigrette, barbecue sauce, and Dijon mustard in a bowl.
2. Keep ¼ cup of this marinade aside for basting later.
3. Add beef cubes to the remaining marinade and toss well to coat.
4. Thread the beef and tomatoes on the skewers, alternately.
5. Set a grill over medium heat and grease its grilling grates.
6. Grill the skewers for 9 minutes while basting them with reserved marinade while flipping every 3 minutes.
7. Serve warm.

Waffle Fries

Serves: 6
Nutritional Information (per serving):
Calories: 216 | Carbs: 25g | Fats: 14g | Protein: 10g

Ingredients

- 2 cups waffle-cut fries, frozen
- ½ teaspoons steak seasoning
- ½ cup shredded cheddar cheese
- 1 tablespoon green onions, chopped
- 1 tablespoon real bacon bits

Directions:

1. Spread the waffle cut fries in a grease 15x10 inches baking pan.
2. Bake these fries for 25 minutes at 450 degrees F in the oven.
3. Drizzle steak seasoning, cheddar cheese, and bacon bits on top.
4. Bake for another 2 minutes, then garnish with green onions.
5. Enjoy.

BBQ Bacon Burger

Serves: 6
Nutritional Information (per serving):
Calories: 786 | Carbs: 60g | Fats: 39g | Protein: 42g

Ingredients

- 12 frozen onion rings
- 2 lbs. ground beef
- 1/4 teaspoon garlic salt
- 1/4 teaspoon black pepper
- 6 slices pepper jack cheese
- 6 hamburger buns, split and toasted
- 1 cup barbecue sauce
- 6 cooked bacon strips

Directions:

1. Prepare and bake the onion rings according to the package's directions.
2. Meanwhile, mix the ground beef with black pepper and garlic salt in a bowl.
3. Make 6 (3/4inches) thick patties out of this mixture.
4. Set a large iron skillet over medium heat and grease it with cooking oil.
5. Sear the beef patties for 7 minutes per side.
6. Add each patty to a burger bun along with onion rings, cheese slice, bacon strips, and barbecue sauce.
7. Serve.

Bacon-Tomato Salad

Serves: 8
Nutritional Information (per serving):
Calories: 268| Carbs: 11g | Fats: 20g | Protein: 10g

Ingredients

- 1 package (12 oz.) iceberg lettuce blend
- 2 cups grape tomatoes, halved
- 3/4 cup coleslaw salad dressing
- 3/4 cup shredded cheddar cheese
- 12 bacon strips, cooked and crumbled

Directions:

1. Toss iceberg lettuce, tomatoes, coleslaw, cheddar cheese in a salad bowl.
2. Garnish with crumbled bacon.
3. Serve.

BBQ Pork Ribs

Serves: 10
Nutritional Information (per serving):
Calories: 483 | Carbs: 31g | Fats: 27g | Protein: 30g

Ingredients

- 2 racks pork baby back ribs
- 1/4 cup soy sauce
- 1/4 cup dried oregano
- 2 tablespoons onion powder
- 2 teaspoons garlic powder
- 1-liter lemon-lime soda
- 1/2 cup unsweetened pineapple

BARBECUE SAUCE
- 1/2 cup hot water
- 1 cup ketchup
- 1/4 cup honey mustard
- 1/2 cup brown sugar
- 1/4 cup barbecue sauce
- 3 tablespoons lemon juice
- 1-1/2 teaspoons white vinegar

Directions:

1. Rub the ribs with soy sauce in a baking tray.
2. Mix garlic powder, onion powder, and oregano in a small bowl.
3. Rub the ribs with this mixture over the ribs and place them in a roasting pan.
4. Cover and refrigerate the ribs overnight.
5. At 225 degrees F, preheat the oven.
6. Add lemon-lime soda to the ribs, cover, and bake for 3 hours until soft.
7. Meanwhile, prepare the BBQ sauce by mixing water, sugar, ketchup, mustard, BBQ sauce, lemon juice, and white vinegar.
8. Mix and cook this mixture until the sauce thickens.
9. Set a grill over medium heat and grease its grilling grates with cooking oil.
10. Brush the ribs with the barbecue sauce.
11. Grill the ribs for 10 minutes per side.
12. Slice and serve warm.

Rattlesnake Bites

Serves: 8
Nutritional Information (per serving):
Calories: 201 | Carbs: 22g | Fats: 11g | Protein: 3g

Ingredients

- 2 cups cornmeal
- 1 egg
- 1 cup 3 tablespoons all-purpose flour
- 2 teaspoons baking powder
- 1-1/2 teaspoons sugar
- 1 teaspoon salt
- 1/2 teaspoon baking soda
- 2/3 cup water
- 1/2 cup buttermilk
- 1/2 cup butter, melted
- 1 cup grated onion
- 2 jalapeno peppers, seeded and chopped
- 1 small green pepper, chopped
- Oil for deep-fat frying

Directions:

1. Mix cornmeal with sugar, salt, baking soda, flour, and baking powder in a bowl.
2. Beat egg with buttermilk, butter, and water in another bowl.
3. Add onion, green pepper, and jalapenos to the egg mixture.
4. Mix well and slowly stir in flour mixture.
5. Mix well until it makes an even cornmeal batter.
6. Add cooking oil to a deep fryer and heat it at 375 degrees F.
7. Drop a teaspoonful of batter into the hot oil, one after another.
8. Deep fry these hush puppies until golden brown.
9. Transfer the fried bites to a plate lined with a paper towel using a slotted spoon.
10. Serve warm.

Ginger-Glazed Grilled Salmon

Serves: 4
Nutritional Information (per serving):
Calories: 299 | Carbs: 8g | Fats: 16g | Protein: 29g

Ingredients

- 2 tablespoons reduced-sodium soy sauce
- 2 tablespoons maple syrup
- 2 teaspoons minced fresh ginger root
- 2 garlic cloves, minced
- 4 (6 oz.) salmon fillets

Directions:

1. Mix soy sauce with maple syrup, ginger root, and garlic in a bowl.
2. Rub this mixture over the fish liberally.
3. Set a grill over medium heat and grease its grilling grates with cooking oil.
4. Grill the glazed salmon for 5 minutes per side while basting it with the remaining marinade.
5. Serve warm.

Texas Peach Fuzz Drink

Serves: 1
Nutritional Information (per serving):
Calories: 200 | Carbs: 11g | Fats: 0.1g | Protein: 0.4g

Ingredients

- 1 1/2 oz. vodka
- 3/4 oz. peach schnapps
- 1/2 oz. creme de cassis
- 2 oz. orange juice
- 2 oz. cranberry juice
- Garnish: orange slice
- Garnish: maraschino cherry

Directions:

1. Add all the liquid ingredients to a drink shaker.
2. Shake well and pour into a serving glass filled with ice.
3. To serve, garnish with a cherry or an orange slice.
4. Enjoy.

Bacon Potato Mash

Serves: 8
Nutritional Information (per serving):
Calories: 130 | Carbs: 5.2g | Fats: 9g | Protein: 7g

Ingredients

- 2 ½ lbs. baby Yukon Gold potatoes
- 1 cup 2% milk, warmed
- 1/2 cup spreadable garlic and herb cream cheese
- 3 tablespoons butter, softened
- 1 lb. bacon strips, cooked and crumbled
- 1 cup shredded cheddar cheese
- 1/2 cup shredded Parmesan cheese
- 3 green onions, chopped
- 1/3 cup oil-packed sun-dried tomatoes, chopped
- 2 teaspoons dried parsley flakes
- 1/4 teaspoon salt
- 1/4 teaspoon black pepper

Directions:

1. Add Yukon potatoes and enough water to cover them in a cooking pot.
2. Cook the potatoes to boil then let them simmer for 20 minutes until soft.
3. Drain the boiled potatoes and mash them in a mixing bowl.
4. Stir in milk, butter, and cream cheese and mix well until evenly incorporated.
5. Add cheeses, green onions, parsley, tomatoes, black pepper, salt, and bacon.
6. Mix well and serve.

Lemony Shrimp with Arugula Sauce

Serves: 6
Nutritional Information (per serving):
Calories: 147 | Carbs: 6g | Fats: 5g | Protein: 20g

Ingredients

- 1/3 cup lemon juice
- 2 tablespoons olive oil
- 2 garlic cloves, minced
- 1/2 teaspoon grated lemon zest
- 1 lb. jumbo shrimp, peeled and deveined
- 2/3 cup fresh arugula
- 2 green onions, sliced
- 1/4 cup plain yogurt
- 2 teaspoons 2% milk
- 1 teaspoon cider vinegar
- 1 teaspoon Dijon mustard
- 1/2 teaspoon sugar
- 1/2 teaspoon salt, divided
- 12 cherry tomatoes
- 1/4 teaspoon black pepper

Directions:

1. Whisk lemon juice, garlic, lemon zest, and oil in a large bowl.
2. Stir in shrimp and toss well to coat, then leave them for 10 minutes.
3. Blend arugula with yogurt, green onions, vinegar, milk, sugar, mustard, and ¼ salt in a food processor until smooth.
4. Thread the tomatoes and shrimp on the skewers, alternately.
5. Drizzle salt and black pepper over the skewers.
6. Set a grill over medium-high heat and grill the skewers for 3 minutes per side.
7. Serve with arugula sauce.

Chicken with Mushroom Sauce

Serves:4
Nutritional Information (per serving):
Calories: 225 | Carbs: 8g | Fats: 9g | Protein: 26g

Ingredients

- 2 teaspoons cornstarch
- 1/2 cup fat-free milk
- 4 (4 oz.) chicken breast, boneless and halved
- 1 tablespoon olive oil
- 1 tablespoon butter
- 1/2 lb. sliced fresh mushrooms
- 1/2 medium onion, thinly sliced
- 1/4 cup sherry or chicken broth
- 1/2 teaspoon salt
- 1/8 teaspoon black pepper

Directions:

1. Place the chicken halves in between plastic wrap and lb. It into ¼ inches thickness.
2. Whisk cornstarch with milk in a bowl until smooth.
3. Set a large iron skillet over medium heat and add oil.
4. Sear the chicken for 6 minutes per side then transfer to a plate.
5. Add butter, onion, and mushrooms to the same pan.
6. Sauté until soft, then add black pepper, salt, and sherry.
7. Cook the sauce to a boil then add cornstarch mixture.
8. Stir and cook for 2 minutes until the sauce thickens.
9. Return the chicken the sauce and cook for 2 minutes.
10. Serve warm.

Cactus Blossom

Serves: 2
Nutritional Information (per serving):
Calories: 65 | Carbs: 11g | Fats: 2g | Protein: 3.5g

Ingredients

- 2 large sweet onions
- 1 tablespoon butter, melted
- 2 teaspoons Dijon mustard
- 3 tablespoons dry bread crumbs
- 1/4 teaspoon salt
- 1/4 teaspoon pepper

SAUCE

- 1/4 cup fat-free sour cream
- 1/4 cup fat-free mayonnaise
- 1-1/2 teaspoons dried minced onion
- 1/4 teaspoon garlic powder
- 1/4 teaspoon dill weed

Directions:

1. Remove ½ inches top of the onions and peel them. Cut each onion into 16 wedges without cutting them from the base. The onions must look like a blooming flower.
2. Place each onion in a 12 inches square foil sheet. And loosely wrap it around the onion.
3. Arrange all the foiled onions in a baking dish and bake for 20 minutes at 425 degrees F.
4. Meanwhile, mix butter with mustard.
5. Unwrap the onions and Brush them with butter mixture.
6. Drizzle black pepper, salt, and bread crumbs on top.
7. Bake the onions for 22 minutes in the oven.
8. Meanwhile, whisk all the ingredients for the sauce in a bowl.
9. Serve the onions with the sauce.

Fried Chicken

Serves: 4
Nutritional Information (per serving):
Calories: 469 | Carbs: 16g | Fats: 28g | Protein: 38g

Ingredients

- 1 large egg
- 1 cup 2% milk
- 2 cups mashed potato flakes
- 1 tablespoon garlic powder
- 1 tablespoon dried oregano
- 1 tablespoon parsley flakes
- 1 tablespoon minced onion
- 1/2 teaspoon salt
- 1/4 teaspoon ground pepper
- 4 (6 oz.) chicken breast, boneless and halved
- Oil for frying

Directions:

1. Whisk and beat egg with 1 cup milk in a shallow bowl.
2. Mix potato flakes with seasonings in a shallow bowl.
3. Reserve half these flakes mixture aside.
4. Place the chicken in between a plastic wrap and lb. It into ½ inches thickness.
5. Dip the chicken halves in egg mixture, then coat with potato flakes mixture and press them.
6. Place the coated chicken in a baking sheet greased with cooking oil.
7. Cover the coated chicken halves and refrigerate for 1 hour.
8. Pour enough oil into a deep fryer and heat it to 350 degrees F.
9. Deep fry the chicken for 5 minutes per side until golden brown.
10. Transfer the crispy golden chicken to a plate lined with paper towels using a slotted spoon.
11. Serve.

Country Chicken with Gravy

Serves: 4
Nutritional Information (per serving):
Calories:274 | Carbs: 20g | Fats: 8g | Protein: 28g

Ingredients

- 3/4 cup crushed cornflakes
- 1/2 teaspoon poultry seasoning
- 1/2 teaspoon paprika
- 1/4 teaspoon salt
- 1/4 teaspoon dried thyme
- 1/4 teaspoon pepper
- 2 tablespoons fat-free evaporated milk
- 4 (4 oz.) chicken breast, boneless and halved
- 2 teaspoons canola oil

GRAVY

- 1 tablespoon butter
- 1 tablespoon all-purpose flour
- 1/4 teaspoon pepper
- 1/8 teaspoon salt
- 1/2 cup fat-free evaporated milk
- 1/4 cup condensed chicken broth, undiluted
- 1 teaspoon sherry or additional condensed chicken broth
- 2 tablespoons minced chives

Directions:

1. Mix cornflakes, poultry seasoning, paprika, salt, thyme, and black pepper in a bowl.
2. Dip the chicken breast in milk and coat them with cornflake mixture.
3. Set a skillet over medium heat and add oil to heat.
4. Sear the coated chicken for 8 minutes per side.
5. Meanwhile, prepare the sauce by melting butter in a saucepan over medium heat.
6. Stir in black pepper, salt, and flour and mix well.
7. Pour in sherry, broth, and milk, then whisk well until smooth and lump-free.
8. Boil the sauce and cook for 2 minutes until it thickens.
9. Serve the chicken with this sauce.

Pulled Pork Sandwiches

Serves: 10
Nutritional Information (per serving):
Calories: 536| Carbs: 66g | Fats: 12g | Protein: 42g

Ingredients

- 1 boneless pork loin roast (4 lbs.), sliced in half
- 1 can (14 ½ oz.) beef broth
- ¾ cup Worcestershire sauce
- 1/2 cup mustard
- ¾ cup Louisiana-style hot sauce
- 1 cup ketchup
- 1 cup molasses
- 10 Kaiser rolls, split

Directions:

1. Mix broth, 1/3 cup hot sauce, and 1/3 cup Worcestershire sauce in a slow cooker.
2. Place the roast in the cooker, cover, and cook for 10 minutes on low heat.
3. Remove the pork from the cooker and shred the pork using two forks.
4. Mix molasses, ketchup, mustard, hot sauce, and Worcestershire sauce in a small bowl.
5. Pour this molasses mixture over the pork and cover again to cook for 30 minutes on high heat.
6. Mix well and divide the pulled in the Kaiser rolls.
7. Enjoy.

Grilled Ribeye with Blue Cheese Mustard Sauce

Serves: 4
Nutritional Information (per serving):
Calories: 547 | Carbs: 3g | Fats: 39g | Protein: 34g

Ingredients

- 1 cup half-and-half cream
- 1/2 cup Dijon mustard
- 1/4 cup 2 teaspoons blue cheese, crumbled
- 1 garlic clove, minced
- 1 tablespoon olive oil
- 1/4 teaspoon salt
- 2 beef ribeye steaks, cut into half, 1 ½ inches thick
- 1/4 teaspoon black pepper

Directions:

1. Mix cream with mustard, garlic, and ¼ cup blue cheese in a small saucepan.
2. Place this pan over low heat with occasional stirring until reduced to half.
3. Season and rub the meat with olive oil, black pepper, and salt.
4. Set a grill over medium heat and grease its grilling grates.
5. Grill the steaks for 6 minutes per side and leave them for 10 minutes on a plate.
6. Pour the blue cheese sauce over the meat and serve with blue cheese on top.
7. Enjoy.

Armadillo Punch

Serves: 1
Nutritional Information (per serving):
Calories: 124 | Carbs: 10g | Fats: 0.1g | Protein: 0.4g

Ingredients

- 1 ¼ oz. coconut rum
- 1 ½ oz. orange juice
- 1 ½ oz. pineapple juice
- Orange slice

Directions:

1. Add all the liquid ingredients to a drink shaker.
2. Shake well and pour into a serving glass filled with ice.
3. Garnish with an orange slice.
4. Serve.

Kenny's Cooler

Serves: 2
Nutritional Information (per serving):
Calories: 98 | Carbs: 9g | Fats: 0g | Protein: 0.1g

Ingredients

- 1 ¼ oz. Coconut rum
- ¾ oz. peach schnapps
- ½ oz. non-alcoholic blue curacao syrup
- ½ oz. sweet and sour mix
- 6 oz. lemonade
- Cherry and orange slice

Directions:

1. Add all the liquid ingredients to a drink shaker.
2. Shake well and pour into a serving glass filled with ice.
3. To serve, garnish with a cherry or an orange slice.
4. Enjoy.

Jamaican Cowboy

Serves: 2
Nutritional Information (per serving):
Calories: 81 | Carbs: 3.3g | Fats: 0g | Protein: 0.2g

Ingredients

- 1 oz. Tequila
- ½ oz. Peach schnapps
- ½ oz. coconut rum
- 1 oz. orange juice
- 1 oz. pineapple juice
- 3 oz. margarita mix
- Orange slice

Directions:

1. Add all the liquid ingredients to a drink shaker.
2. Shake well and pour into a serving glass filled with ice.
3. Garnish with an orange slice.
4. Serve.

Sangria Red

Serves: 2
Nutritional Information (per serving):
Calories: 140 | Carbs: 17g | Fats: 0g | Protein: 0.6g

Ingredients

- 3 ½ oz. red wine
- 2 ½ oz. orange juice
- ½ oz. sweet and sour
- ½ oz. grenadine
- ½ oz. triple sec
- ½ oz. peach puree
- ½ oz. brandy
- Splash of Sprite
- Lime wedge, cherry, orange slice

Directions:

1. Add all the liquid ingredients to a drink shaker.
2. Shake well and pour into a serving glass filled with ice.
3. Garnish with a cherry, lime wedge, and orange slice.
4. Serve.

Hurricane Margarita

Serves: 3
Nutritional Information (per serving):
Calories: 139 | Carbs: 24g | Fats: 0g | Protein: 0.1g

Ingredients

- 1 oz. tequila
- 1 oz. Captain Morgan Spiced Rum
- 1 oz. OJ
- 1 oz. pineapple juice
- 3 oz. grenadine
- 3 oz. margarita mix
- Orange slice and cherry

Directions:

1. Add all the liquid ingredients to a drink shaker.
2. Shake well and pour into serving glasses filled with ice.
3. Use an orange slice or a cherry to garnish the drink.
4. Serve.

Texas Strawberry Margarita

Serves: 4
Nutritional Information (per serving):
Calories: 103 | Carbs: 8g | Fats: 0g | Protein: 0.1g

Ingredients

- 3 oz. tequila
- 1 oz. triple sec
- 8 oz. frozen strawberries
- 2 oz. frozen limeade concentrate
- 1/2 tablespoon sugar
- Kosher or sea salt

Directions:

1. Add all the strawberries, sugar, salt, ice, and liquid ingredients to a blender.
2. Blend well and pour the drink into the serving glasses filled with crushed ice.
3. Mix well and serve.

Texas Roadhouse Loaded Sweet Potato

Serves: 1
Nutritional Information (per serving):
Calories: 279 | Carbs: 42g | Fats: 12g | Protein: 2g

Ingredients

- 1 small/medium sweet potato
- 1 tablespoon melted butter
- 1 tablespoon brown sugar
- 1 teaspoon vanilla extract
- A dash of cinnamon
- ¼ cup marshmallows

Directions:

4. At 400 degrees F, preheat your oven.
5. Rinse and pat dry all the sweet potatoes and prick them with a fork.
6. Place these potatoes in a baking tray, lined with a parchment paper.
7. Bake the potatoes for 50 minutes in the preheated oven.
8. Mix melted butter with brown sugar, vanilla extract, and cinnamon in a mixing bowl.
9. Drizzle the butter mixture over the potatoes.
10. Carve a slit on top of the potatoes and stuff them with marshmallows.
11. Drizzle butter mixture on top.
12. Broil the potatoes for 1 minute in the oven.
13. Serve warm.

Strawberry Cheesecake

Serves: 8
Nutritional Information (per serving):
Calories: 322 | Carbs: 32g | Fats: 19g | Protein: 6g

Ingredients

Crust

- 2 cups graham cracker crumbs
- 1/4 cup granulated sugar
- 6 tablespoons butter, melted

Filling

- 32 oz. cream cheese
- 1 1/3 cups granulated sugar
- 1 cup sour cream
- 1 tablespoon vanilla extract
- 1/4 teaspoon salt
- 4 large eggs, lightly beaten

Sauce

- 16 oz. whole strawberries, diced
- 2 tablespoons cornstarch
- 1 cup granulated sugar
- 2 teaspoons vanilla extract
- 1/8 teaspoon salt
- 2 cups strawberries, finely chopped

Directions

1. At 350 degrees F, preheat your oven. Grease a 9 inches springform pan with aluminum foil.
2. Blend graham crumbs with melted butter and sugar in a food processor.
3. Spread this mixture in the prepared pan, press the mixture and bake for 10 minutes.
4. Switch the oven temperature to 300 degrees F.
5. Beat and whisk the cream cheese in a mixing bowl for 1 minute using an electric mixer until creamy and smooth.
6. Stir in sour cream and sugar, then beat well until well incorporated.
7. Add salt and vanilla then continue beating on low speed until smooth.
8. Stir in eggs, mix well and pour the batter into the baked crust.
9. Pour boiling water into the roasting pan and place the cheesecake pan in the water.

10. Bake the cheesecake about 1 hour in the preheated oven.
11. Remove the cake from the roasting pan and allow it to cool.
12. Prepare the sauce:
13. Blend whole strawberries with cornstarch in a food processor until smooth
14. Transfer this puree to a saucepan and cook on medium heat.
15. Stir in sugar and cook for 15 minutes with occasional stirring until it thickens.
16. Add salt, chopped strawberries, and vanilla then mix well.
17. Allow the sauce to cool, then mix occasionally.
18. Spread this sauce on top of the cheesecake.
19. Refrigerate this cake for 4 hours.
20. Slice and serve.

Texas Roadhouse Rolls

Serves: 12
Nutritional Information (per serving):
Calories: 215 | Carbs: 35g | Fats: 6g | Protein: 5g

Ingredients

- 1 cup warm milk
- 1 1/8 teaspoon active yeast
- 1/3 cup sugar
- 3 1/2 cups all-purpose flour
- 1 egg
- 1/3 cup butter melted
- 1 teaspoon salt

Directions:

1. Mix warm milk with yeast and sugar in a small bowl. Leave it for 5 minutes.
2. Blend flour with egg, salt, and 1/3 cup melted butter in a food processor.
3. Stir in milk mixture then mix until it makes a smooth dough.
4. Transfer this dough to a bowl and cover it with a plastic wrap. Leave this dough for 2 hours at a warm place in the kitchen.
5. Knead this dough for another 10 minutes and roll this dough into ½ inch thick sheet on a floured surface.
6. Cut this dough into 16 portions and place these portions in a baking pan, greased with cooking oil.
7. Leave these pieces for 30 minutes at room temperature.
8. At 375 degrees F, preheat the oven.
9. Bake the rolls for 10 minutes in the preheated oven.
10. Meanwhile, brush the rolls with ¼ cup melted butter.
11. Serve.

Roadhouse Baked Potato

Serves: 2
Nutritional Information (per serving):
Calories: 129 | Carbs: 31g | Fats: 0.2g | Protein: 4g

Ingredients

- 1 teaspoon sea salt, to taste
- 2 large baking potatoes
- 2 tablespoons bacon fat
- Shredded cheddar cheese, to garnish
- Sour cream
- Chives
- Bacon bits
- Mrs. Dash seasoning

Directions:

1. Spread 2 foil pieces on a flat surface and place the potato skins on it.
2. Drizzle bacon fat and sea salt on top of the potatoes.
3. Wrap the foil sheet around the potatoes and bake for 45 minutes at 425 degrees F.
4. Serve the baked potatoes with cheddar cheese, sour cream, chives, Mrs. Dash seasoning, and bacon bits.
5. Enjoy.

Rattlesnake Margarita

Serves: 1
Nutritional Information (per serving):
Calories: 129 | Carbs: 3g | Fats: 0g | Protein: 0g

Ingredients

- Juice of 1/4 Lime
- 1 ½ oz. Sour mix
- 1 oz. cranberry juice
- 1/2 oz. raspberry liqueur
- 1 oz. Tequila

Directions:

1. Add all the liquid ingredients to a drink shaker.
2. Shake well and pour into serving glasses filled with ice.
3. Serve.

Apple Pie

Serves: 8
Nutritional Information (per serving):
Calories: 320 | Carbs: 13g | Fats: 56g | Protein: 1.1g

Ingredients

- 9-inch double-crust pie
- ½ cup unsalted butter
- 3 tablespoons all-purpose flour
- ¼ cup of water
- ½ cup white sugar
- ½ cup packed brown sugar
- 8 medium apples, peeled, cored, and sliced

Directions:

1. At 425 degrees F, preheat the oven.
2. Add unsalted butter to a saucepan and melt it.
3. Stir in flour and mix well to make a paste.
4. Add brown sugar, white sugar, and water, then cook this mixture to a boil.
5. Cook this mixture on a simmer.
6. Spread the double pie crust in a pie plate.
7. Pour the sugar filling into the crust and top it with apple slices.
8. Bake the pie for 15 minutes in the preheated oven.
9. Reduce the oven's heat to 350 degrees F.
10. Bake it for almost 45 minutes in the oven.
11. Slice and serve warm.

Smothered Chicken

Serves: 4
Nutritional Information (per serving):
Calories: 213 | Carbs: 11g | Fats: 8g | Protein: 26g

Ingredients

- 3 chicken breasts
- 1 tablespoon olive oil
- 2 teaspoon minced garlic
- 2 lbs mushrooms, sliced
- 1 large onion
- 1 teaspoon Greek seasoning
- 2 tablespoons corn starch
- 1/2 cup chicken broth

Directions:

1. Horizontally, cut the chicken breasts in half and season them with black pepper and salt.
2. Grill the chicken in a preheated grill for 5 minutes per side until golden brown.
3. Sauté garlic with oil in a wok for 1 minute.
4. Toss in sliced veggies, Greek seasoning, and sauté for 8 minutes.
5. Mix 2 tbsp cornstarch with 1 tablespoon water in a bowl and pour it into the wok.
6. Stir and cook the chicken until it thickens.
7. Serve the grilled chicken with the prepared sauce on top.
8. Serve warm.

Chicken with Portobello Mushrooms

Serves: 4
Nutritional Information (per serving):
Calories: 340 | Carbs: 1.5g | Fats: 17g | Protein: 42g

Ingredients

- 1 tablespoon olive oil
- 4 boneless, skinless chicken breasts
- 1 cup chicken broth
- 1 tablespoon roasted garlic paste
- 2 cups portobello mushrooms, sliced
- ½ teaspoon dried thyme leaves
- 1 tablespoon butter

Directions:

1. Sear chicken breasts with olive oil in a skillet for 5 minutes per side.
2. Stir in roasted garlic paste and chicken broth.
3. Cover and cook the chicken garlic mixture for 10 minutes on a low simmer.
4. During this time, sauté mushrooms with thyme and butter in a saucepan.
5. Cook for about 2 minutes, then transfer this mixture to the chicken.
6. Cook for 2 minutes then serve warm.
7. Enjoy.

Herb Crusted Chicken Breast

Serves: 1
Nutritional Information (per serving):
Calories: 154 | Carbs: 0g | Fats: 7g | Protein: 21g

Ingredients

- 1 boneless, skinless chicken breast
- 1 teaspoon olive oil
- 1 teaspoon Herbes de Provence
- 1/4 teaspoon Kosher salt
- Garlic powder, to taste

Directions:

1. At 350 degrees F, preheat your oven.
2. Brush the chicken breast with oil, garlic powder, Herbes de proves, and salt.
3. Sear the seasoned chicken for 4 minutes per side in a skillet, greased with olive oil.
4. Transfer this skillet to the oven and bake the chicken for 14 minutes.
5. Slice and serve warm.

Grilled BBQ Chicken

Serves: 8
Nutritional Information (per serving):
Calories: 523 | Carbs: 17g | Fats: 20g | Protein: 66g

Ingredients

Sauce

- 2 tablespoons vegetable oil
- 1/4 cup onion, minced
- 1/2 cup white vinegar
- 1 1/2 cups water
- 1/2 cup tomato paste
- 1/2 cup brown sugar
- 2 tablespoons honey
- 1 tablespoon Worcestershire sauce
- 1 3/4 teaspoon salt
- 1 teaspoon bourbon whiskey
- 1 teaspoon liquid smoke
- 1/8 teaspoon garlic powder
- 1/8 teaspoon paprika
- 1/4 teaspoon black pepper, freshly ground

Chicken

- 4 pounds chicken pieces
- Salt, to taste
- Vegetable oil
- 1 cup barbecue sauce

Directions:

1. Brush the chicken pieces with oil and salt and grill them for 5 minutes per side in a preheated grill.
2. Move this chicken to the side of the grill, reduce the heat to medium-low, cover, and cook for 30 minutes.
3. Now flip the chicken and baste it with barbecue sauce.
4. Cook the chicken for another 30 minutes. Brush them with barbecue sauce.
5. Flip and cooking again for 30 minutes.
6. Serve warm.

Roadhouse Burger

Serves: 4
Nutritional Information (per serving):
Calories: 628 | Carbs: 37g | Fats: 36g | Protein: 38g

Ingredients

- 1 1/2lbs ground beef
- Salt and black pepper, to taste
- 4 slices Swiss cheese
- 8 slices bacon
- 4 onion hamburger buns
- 4 large frozen onion rings
- 2 large onions, thinly sliced

Garlic Mayonnaise:

- 6 tablespoons mayonnaise
- 2 garlic cloves, pressed
- 1 teaspoon fresh lemon juice
- 1 teaspoon extra virgin olive oil

Directions:

1. Whisk mayonnaise with lemon juice, garlic, salt, black pepper, and 1 teaspoon olive oil in a small bowl, then cover and refrigerate.
2. Pour cooking oil into a deep fryer and heat to 375 degrees F.
3. Deep the fry onion rings until golden brown, then transfer to a plate lined with a paper towel.
4. Sauté onion slices with remaining oil in a skillet over medium heat, cover, and cook for 30 minutes on medium heat until caramelized.
5. Remove the lid and add ½ cup water and cook for 5 minutes. Set this onion aside.
6. Sauté bacon until crispy, then transfer to a plate, lined with a paper towel.
7. Prepare 4 patties out of the beef mixture and grill them for 5 minutes per side on a grill over medium heat.
8. Place one Swiss cheese slice on top of each patty and allow the cheese to melt.
9. Place the patties in the buns, bacon, caramelized onions, onion rings.
10. Top the patties with garlic mayo.
11. Serve.

Texas Roadhouse Pork Ribs

Serves: 8
Nutritional Information (per serving):
Calories: 422 | Carbs: 17g | Fats: 30g | Protein: 20g

Ingredients

- 1 slab pork loin rib, frozen
- 1/4 cup Texas roadhouse rib seasoning
- 2 1/2 cups water
- 1/2 cup liquid smoke
- 2 tablespoons vegetable oil
- 1/4 cup minced fresh onion
- 1 1/2 cups water
- 1/2 cup tomato paste
- 1/2 cup white vinegar
- 1/2 cup brown sugar
- 2 tablespoons honey
- 1 tablespoon Worcestershire sauce
- 1 3/4 teaspoons salt
- 1 teaspoon liquid smoke
- 1 teaspoon whiskey
- 1/4 teaspoon black pepper
- 1/8 teaspoon garlic powder
- 1/8 teaspoon paprika

Directions:

1. At 275 degrees F, preheat the oven. Place a wire rack on a large pan.
2. Place the ribs on the wire rack and rub the ribs with Texas roadhouse rib seasoning liberally.
3. Mix liquid smoke and water in a bowl and pour it in the large pan.
4. Cover the ribs with the aluminum foil and bake them or 5 hours.
5. Meanwhile, sauté onion with vegetable oil in a cooking pot until soft.
6. Stir in remaining ingredients and cook until the mixture thickens.
7. Preheat a gas grill on medium heat and grill the ribs for 4 minutes per side.
8. Serve the ribs with the prepared sauce.
9. Enjoy.

Roadhouse Steak Rub

Serves: 8
Nutritional Information (per serving):
Calories: 6 | Carbs: 1.4g | Fats: 0g | Protein: 0.1g

Ingredients

- 2 teaspoons coarse kosher salt
- 2 teaspoons brown sugar
- 1/4 teaspoon cornstarch
- 1/4 teaspoon garlic powder
- 1/4 teaspoon garlic salt
- 1/4 teaspoon onion powder
- 1/4 teaspoon turmeric
- 1/2 teaspoon paprika
- 1/2 teaspoon chili powder
- 1 teaspoon black pepper

Directions:

1. Mix and whisk all the steak rub's ingredients in a clean bowl.
2. Store and seal the rubs in a mason jar.

Chicken Critters

Serves: 6
Nutritional Information (per serving):
Calories: 348 | Carbs: 38g | Fats: 8.2g | Protein: 291g

Ingredients

- 12 chicken tenders
- 4 large eggs
- 3 cup all-purpose flour
- 4 tablespoon lemon pepper seasoning

Directions:

1. Beat eggs in one bowl and mix all-purpose flour with lemon pepper seasoning in another bowl.
2. Coat the chicken tenders with flour mixture, dip them in the egg's mixture, and coat again with flour mixture.
3. Pour cooking oil into a deep-frying pan and heat it to 350 degrees F.
4. Deep fry the tenders until golden brown.
5. Serve warm.

Baked Steak Fries

Serves: 2
Nutritional Information (per serving):
Calories: 222 | Carbs: 37g | Fats: 7g | Protein: 4.1g

Ingredients

- 1 lb. russet potatoes
- 1 tablespoon cooking oil
- 1/2 tablespoon paprika
- 1/2 tablespoon steak seasoning

Directions:

1. At 425 degrees F, preheat the oven.
2. Cut the russet potatoes into wedges and transfer them to a bowl.
3. Stir in cooking oil, paprika, and steak seasoning.
4. Toss well and spread them in a baking sheet lined with parchment paper.
5. Bake the potatoes for 35 minutes.
6. Serve warm.

Applesauce

Serves: 12
Nutritional Information (per serving):
Calories: 71 | Carbs: 19g | Fats: 0.2g | Protein: 0.2g

Ingredients

- 4 pounds of apples, cored and peeled
- 2 strips of lemon peel
- 3 tablespoons lemon juice
- 1/2 teaspoon ground cinnamon
- 1/2 cup of white sugar
- 1 cup of water
- 1/2 teaspoon of salt

Directions:

1. Add apples to a large pot and stir in lemon juice, lemon peel, sugar, cinnamon, 1 cup water, and salt to a cooking pot.
2. Place it over high heat, let it boil, then cook on low heat for 20 minutes.
3. Remove the lemon peels from the water.
4. Puree the soft apple mixture with a masher or hand blender until smooth.
5. Allow the applesauce to cool.
6. Serve.

Buttery Seasoned Rice

Serves: 6
Nutritional Information (per serving):
Calories: 281 | Carbs: 51g | Fats: 6g | Protein: 5g

Ingredients

- 2 cups long-grain white rice, uncooked
- 3 1/4 cups water
- 2 teaspoon chicken powder
- 1 teaspoon garlic powder
- 1 teaspoon onion powder
- 1 teaspoon paprika
- 1/2 teaspoon dried thyme
- 2 tablespoon dried parsley
- 1 teaspoon salt
- 1/2 teaspoon black pepper
- 3 tablespoon butter, unsalted

Directions:

1. Add white rice, water, chicken powder, garlic powder, onion powder, paprika, dried thyme, parsley, salt, and black pepper to a cooking pot.
2. Cook the rice on medium-low heat for 13 minutes, on a simmer until the water is completely evaporated.
3. Fluff the spicy rice with a fork, then add butter.
4. Mix well and serve warm.

Corn on the cob with garlic butter

Serves: 8
Nutritional Information (per serving):
Calories: 203 | Carbs: 14g | Fats: 14g | Protein: 4.1g

Ingredients

- 4 ears of corn, husks and husks removed
- 4 cups of milk
- 2 cups water
- Salt, to taste

Garlic Butter

- 1/2 cup butter
- 1 clove garlic, crushed
- 2 tablespoons parsley, chopped
- Salt to taste

Directions:

1. Place corn ears in a cooking pot and add water, salt, and milk on top.
2. Boil the corn in the milk, reduce the heat, and cook for 8 minutes.
3. Prepare the garlic butter by mixing its ingredients in a bowl.
4. Transfer the cob to a serving plate.
5. Drizzle garlic butter on top.
6. Serve warm.

Sautéed Onions

Serves: 4
Nutritional Information (per serving):
Calories: 121 | Carbs: 11g | Fats: 9g | Protein: 1.3g

Ingredients

- 3 large onions, sliced
- 3 tablespoons butter
- Pinch kosher salt
- 3 tablespoons sherry

Directions:

1. Mix butter with onions in a frying pan and place it over medium heat.
2. Sauté onion until caramelized, then drizzle salt on top.
3. Pour in the sherry and mix well.
4. Serve.

Texas Roadhouse Rita

Serves: 2
Nutritional Information (per serving):
Calories: 180 | Carbs: 21g | Fats: 0.2g | Protein: 1.5g

Ingredients

- 3 oz. Jose Cuervo Gold Tequila
- ¾ cup sweet and sour mix
- ¾ cup orange juice
- 1 ½ oz. triple sec
- 1 ½ oz. bud light
- Lime wedges, to garnish

Directions:

1. Add all the liquid ingredients to a drink shaker.
2. Shake well and pour into serving glasses filled with ice.
3. Use lime wedges to garnish.
4. Serve.

All-American Cheeseburger Recipe

Serves: 6
Nutritional Information (per serving):
Calories: 443 | Carbs: 44g | Fats: 20g | Protein: 24g

Ingredients

- 2 lbs. freshly ground chuck
- 1 tablespoon onion powder
- 1 teaspoon salt
- 1 teaspoon black pepper
- 12 slices American cheese
- 6 large burger buns, toasted

To garnish

- ketchup
- mayonnaise
- thousand island dressing
- sliced red onion
- sliced tomatoes
- sliced pickles
- fresh lettuce leaves

Directions:

1. Mix beef with salt, black pepper, and onion powder in a large mixing bowl.
2. Make six patties out of this mixture and keep them aside.
3. Set a grill over high heat and grease its grilling grates.
4. Grill the patties for 5 minutes per side.
5. Place the patties in the burgers along with tomato slices, pickles, and lettuce leaves.
6. Serve warm.

Sirloin Fried Steak

Serves: 2
Nutritional Information (per serving):
Calories: 596 | Carbs: 37g | Fats: 33g | Protein: 37g

Ingredients

- ½ pound beef top sirloin steak
- 1/4 cup all-purpose flour
- 1/4 cup seasoned bread crumbs
- 1 egg
- 2 teaspoons water
- 3 tablespoons canola oil

COUNTRY GRAVY

- 2 tablespoons all-purpose flour
- 1-1/4 cups 2% milk
- 1/4 teaspoon salt
- 1/4 teaspoon white pepper

Directions:

1. Pound the steak into ¼ inch thickens and cut it into half.
2. Spread flour in a shallow bowl, and breadcrumbs in another shallow tray.
3. Beat egg with water in another bowl.
4. Coat the steaks with the flour, dip the steaks in the egg mixture and coat them with the crumbs.
5. Sear the coated steaks for 2 minutes per side in a skillet greased with oil until golden brown.
6. Transfer the seared steaks to a plate and keep them aside.
7. Meanwhile, prepare the gravy by adding flour to the same pan.
8. Mix well until blended, then stir in milk. Cook the mixture to a boil.
9. Cook and mix for 2 minutes until the mixture thickens.
10. Add salt and black pepper for seasoning then mix well.
11. Serve the steak with hot sauce on top.

Texas Roadhouse Cinnamon Butter

Serves: 6
Nutritional Information (per serving):
Calories: 252 | Carbs: 13g | Fats: 23g | Protein: 0.3g

Ingredients

- 3/4 cup salted butter, softened
- 1/3 cup powdered sugar
- 2 tablespoon honey
- 1 teaspoon ground cinnamon
- 1/8 teaspoon pure vanilla extract

Directions:

1. Beat butter with honey, sugar, vanilla, and cinnamon in a mixing bowl until completely combined.
2. Transfer to a mason jar, seal the lid, and refrigerate for 1 hour.
3. Serve when chilled.

Chicken Mushrooms Sandwiches

Serves: 4
Nutritional Information (per serving):
Calories: 522 | Carbs: 22g | Fats: 36g | Protein: 31g

Ingredients

- 4 ciabatta rolls, halved horizontally
- 3 tablespoons olive oil
- 1 tablespoon whole grain mustard, to rub
- 8 oz. Fontina cheese, shredded
- 12 oz. white mushrooms, sliced
- 2 tablespoons shallots, chopped
- 3 garlic cloves, pressed
- 2 cups roast chicken, shredded
- 1 5-oz. bag baby spinach

Directions:

1. At 400 degrees F, preheat the oven.
2. Pull the ciabatta rolls to get a hollow center.
3. Brush the ciabatta rolls with olive oil, mustard, and place them in a baking tray.
4. Drizzle half of the fontina cheese on top.
5. Sauté mushrooms with 2 tablespoons oil in a large skillet over medium-high heat for 4 minutes.
6. Stir in garlic and shallots then sauté for 3 minutes.
7. Add roasted and shredded chicken to the skillet and cook for 2 minutes.
8. Transfer the mixture to a plate and keep it aside.
9. Pour 1 tablespoon oil into the same skillet and sauté spinach for 2 minutes.
10. Stir in black pepper and salt, mix well and keep it aside.
11. Divide the chicken mixture in the ciabatta rolls and top them with spinach mixture.
12. Drizzle remaining cheese on top.
13. Bake the rolls for 20 minutes in the oven.
14. Serve warm.

Texas Roadhouse Caesar Salad

Serves: 4
Nutritional Information (per serving):
Calories: 165 | Carbs: 12g | Fats: 12g | Protein: 3.4g

Ingredients

- 1/2 cup mayonnaise
- 1/2 cup parmesan cheese, grated
- 1/4 cup buttermilk
- 1/4 cup sweet and sour dressing
- 2 tablespoons dry Ranch dressing mix
- 1 teaspoon garlic pepper
- 1 garlic clove, minced and mashed

THE SALAD

- 4 cups Romaine lettuce, chopped
- ½ cup fresh shredded Asiago cheese
- ½ cup toasted croutons.

Directions:

1. Whisk and mix all the ingredients for dressing in a salad bowl.
2. Toss in salad ingredients then mix well.
3. Serve.

Classic House Salad

Serves: 4
Nutritional Information (per serving):
Calories: 289 | Carbs: 27g | Fats: 18g | Protein: 9.2g

Ingredients

- 4 cups mixed romaine, cut into bite-sized pieces
- 11/2 cups grape tomatoes
- 1 1/2 cups cucumber, sliced
- 1 cup croutons, toasted
- 3/4 cup red onion, halved and sliced
- 2/3 cup freshly grated cheddar cheese separated
- 1/2 cup salad dressing
- 1/4 cup crispy bacon crumbled

Directions:

1. Whisk and mix all the ingredients for dressing in a salad bowl.
2. Toss in salad ingredients then mix well.
3. Serve.

Texas Roadhouse Cheese Fries

Serves: 4
Nutritional Information (per serving):
Calories: 337 | Carbs: 18g | Fats: 23g | Protein: 17g

Ingredients

- 4 cups frozen steak-style French fries
- 1/4 teaspoon garlic salt
- 1/4 teaspoon seasoning salt
- 1/4 teaspoon onion powder
- 2 cups grated sharp cheddar cheese
- 6 -8 slices bacon
- Cooking oil, for deep frying

Directions:

1. At 450 degrees F, preheat the oven.
2. Sauté bacon in a frying pan on mediumohigh heat until crispy.
3. Transfer them to a plate, lined with a paper towel.
4. Add salt, onion powder, and garlic salt to the bacon grease, mix well and keep it aside.
5. Spread the fries in a greased baking sheet and bake them for 15 minutes until golden brown.
6. Switch the oven to a broiler setting.
7. Drizzle the bacon greased and on top of the fries.
8. Add cheddar cheese, and crumbled bacon top.
9. Broil the fries for 5 minutes in the oven.
10. Serve warm.

Roadhouse Big Ol' Brownie

Serves: 6
Nutritional Information (per serving):
Calories: 134 | Carbs: 22g | Fats: 4.5g | Protein: 1.7g

Ingredients

- 1 box brownie mix
- Vanilla ice cream
- Hot fudge sauce

Directions:

1. At 350 degrees F, preheat the oven.
2. Line a muffin tray with foil strips.
3. Prepare the brownie batter according to the given package's instructions.
4. Divide this batter in the muffin tray and bake them for 40 minutes in the oven.
5. Serve the brownies with ice cream scoops and hot fudge sauce.
6. Enjoy.

Roadhouse Pot Roast

Serves: 4
Nutritional Information (per serving):
Calories: 557 | Carbs: 16g | Fats: 19g | Protein: 65g

Ingredients

- 2 lbs. chuck roast
- 1/2 onion chopped
- 1/2 bell pepper any color, chopped
- 2 stalks celery chopped
- 2 cloves of garlic minced or pressed
- 1/2 cup tomato sauce
- 1/2 cup BBQ sauce
- 2 beef bouillon cubes
- 1 teaspoon salt
- 1 teaspoon black pepper
- 1/2 teaspoon dried thyme
- 1/2 cup water

Directions:

1. Mix onion with bell pepper, garlic, and celery in a mixing bowl.
2. Add chuck roast, spices, water, tomato sauce, and BBQ sauce to the veggies.
3. Toss well, cover, and marinate overnight.
4. Transfer this chuck roast to a slow cooker, cover, and cook for 10 hours on low heat.
5. Serve warm.

Fried Steak

Serves: 4
Nutritional Information (per serving):
Calories: 378 | Carbs: 38g | Fats: 21.3g | Protein: 11g

Ingredients

- 1 1/2 cups flour
- 2 teaspoons kosher salt
- 2 teaspoons freshly ground pepper
- 4 tablespoons paprika
- 2 eggs
- 1/2 cup buttermilk
- 1/2 cup Shiner Bock
- Peanut oil, for cooking
- 4 tenderized round steaks
- 2 cups Cracked-Pepper Gravy

Cracked-Pepper Gravy

- 1/2 cup unsalted butter
- 5 tablespoons flour
- 2 1/2 cups whole milk
- 1 1/2 teaspoons kosher salt
- 4 teaspoons cracked pepper

Directions:

1. Mix flour with salt, black pepper, and paprika in a mixing bowl.
2. Beat eggs with buttermilk and beer in another bowl.
3. In a heavy cooking skillet, heat oil to 350 degrees F.
4. Coat the steaks with flour, dip in the buttermilk mixture, then again coat with flour mixture.
5. Sear the coated steaks for 3 minutes per side until golden brown.
6. Meanwhile, prepare the cracker pepper gravy.
7. Melt butter in a cooking pan and stir in flour.
8. Whisk well, then slowly add milk, salt, and cracked pepper.
9. Stir and cook until the mixture thickens.
10. Pour this sauce over the steaks.
11. Serve warm.

Conclusion

With all the delicious Texas Roadhouse copycat recipes shared in this cookbook, you can make your menu super exciting and fun. Now you don't have to miss out on your favorite Texas Roadhouse tastes just because you can't visit this place. You can enjoy the same restaurant as flavors and aromas while eating healthy home-picked and cooked ingredients. Whether it is the routine breakfast or side salads, appetizers, lunch, dinner, or desserts, you can recreate all the famous Texas recipes at home by using these copycat ideas. These recipes are not only great for cooking lovers, but they are equally recommended to all the beginners who want to surprise others with great aromas.

I have always been a great fan of the Texas Roadhouse original flavors. For quite sometimes, I believed it was almost impossible to recreate those flavors at home. But then I started experimenting with the basics, and with every trial, I came one step closer to the authentic Texas Roadhouse menu. Home-cooking all its famous recipes was not just challenging, but it was also a bit exciting for me. Eating all my favorite meals using organic ingredients at home turned out to be a bliss. And ever since I started sharing my copycat Texas Roadhouse meals with others, there was this huge appeal to share the secrets behind those recipes. So, I have written down all the recipes that I tried, and this cookbook is from my very own Texas Roadhouse personal collection. The spices, seasonings, and all other major ingredients are selected with care and precision to keep the taste up to the mark. Since I am a health enthusiast myself, I made sure to use as many fresh ingredients as possible. These recipes are specially created while keeping everyone's health considerations in mind; whether it's old or the young, we can serve them all.

So, it's about time that you, too, recreate the irresistible Texas Roadhouse flavors at home and share the recipes and this cookbook with your loved ones as well. Any Texas Roadhouse fan would definitely love to have these recipes on the menu.

Made in United States
Troutdale, OR
01/17/2024

16990147R00044